Dried Tears,
A Woman's Guide to Overcoming

You are an Overcomer!
Love,
Jennifer
Jer 29:11

GODZCHILD PUBLICATIONS

© 2011 Godzchild, Inc.

Published by Godzchild Publications
a division of Godzchild, Inc.
22 Halleck St., Newark, NJ 07104
www.godzchildproductions.net

Printed in the United States of America 2011— First Edition
Cover Design by Leonard Poteat
Editor Erica Pitts

Library of Congress Cataloging-in-Publications Data
Dried Tears: A Woman's Guide to Overcoming/Jennifer Lucy. Includes a   journal.

ISBN   978-0-9840955-7-5 (pbk.)
        978-1-937095-38-3 (EPUB)
        978-1-937095-39-0 (EPDF)

1. Lucy, Jennifer. 2. Inspirational. 3. Christianity. 4. Journal.

2011924035

Dedication

This book is dedicated to my Goddaughter Zaelyn Amore Watson because I have decreed that she will be a powerful woman of God as she grows up! I also dedicate this book to my mom for being the powerful woman of God you are and inspiring me!

Table of Contents

Dried Tears

~A WOMAN'S GUIDE TO OVERCOMING~

Endorsements

Official Website of
TY ADAMS

Ty Adams Int'l 20318 Grand River Detroit, MI 48219
www.iTy.TV ~ www.TyAdams.org

If you're going through or have ever been in emotional or relationship trauma, then you know what it feels like to be broken and crushed, curled up in a knot, in a fetal position, to the point of tears, and it feels as if the endless pain will never go away! Reading through the pages of Dried Tears, I knew emphatically that Jennifer Lucy had gone through and has overcome the tears that accompany pain and brokenness because it was as if she was telling my story. Get ready to dry your tears! As you curl up with this book, it'll untangle you out of the pain of your past as you journey through healing with the turn of every page!

Ty Adams,
international speaker and
best-selling author of *Single, Saved &
Having Sex* and *How To Date With
Your Clothes On*

Sexual Purity With Contemporary Style and Urban Class
http://www.iamworththewait.com/wtwr/

Why struggle with the challenges of sexual sin: the thoughts, the toxic relationships, and the destructive behaviors? Jennifer's story is real, but her reality of overcoming, is even more real. Become an overcomer! Read this book and be inspired! Read this book and be healed!

Dr. Lindsay Marsh Warren
President
Worth The Wait Revolution, Inc

Foreword

For years it has been my desire to see women fulfill their God-given purpose and to be "happy." There are too many women that allow situations and circumstances to hinder them from receiving all that God has for them. There was a time in my life where I would say, "I just want to be happy!" Today, this is my reality. Anything is possible to those that would "believe" and "apply" Biblical principles into their daily life.

I have watched Jennifer grow and develop throughout her years of attending Spirit of Faith Christian Center. She is a true believer who has learned to not only hear the Word of God, but to apply it in her life. Jennifer's testimony is one of overcoming various odds. No matter what her situations have been in life, she has learned to dry the tears and focus on the prize set before her!

In this book, not only will you learn more about her ability to overcome sexual perversion, drugs, low self esteem, etc., you will receive tips that will assist you with overcoming anything in your life that's hindering you from walking in purpose! Jennifer's frank and sometimes humorous approach will compel you to want to read more and more. If you will embrace the principles of the Word of God in this book, you will indeed be an "OVERCOMER" in every area of your life!

~Dee Dee Freeman

Introduction

My praise is everlasting! My praise is lifted from the very depths of my soul! I praise God consistently, not only for sending His Beloved Son to die for my sins, but for keeping His Spirit alive in me even when I lived in sin. He's replaced my spirit of heaviness with a garment of praise! He's dried my tears of pain and replaced them with smiles and tears of joy!

Growing up attending Abundant Life Faith Bible Church in Takoma Park, MD and surrounded by the biblical teachings of my aunt in our home, seeds were planted. It is because of those "word seeds," coupled with the mercy of God and the prayers of my family, friends, and Spirit of Faith Christian Center intercessors, that I am alive today.

During my early childhood I absolutely loved church. In my home, if we didn't physically get up and go to church, my aunt would wake me up along with her four children to have "Children's church." There was no way for us to escape getting the Word of God. Besides, I never wanted to because I truly enjoyed learning and hearing the stories of Jesus,

Noah, Moses, Joseph, Adam and Eve, etc. It was in those intimate family services that the spiritual foundation of my heart was being laid. And then I grew up...

As all of my aunt's children grew older, we became more and more crowded in the home we lived in. At fourteen years old, my mom, dad and I moved into another home with just the three of us. I was excited because I would finally experience privacy, something I never had growing up in a home with 11 people. At the time, my parents were not saved, so the door was open for Satan to take reign in our lives. During my teenage years, the doors of sin became very evident in my life and I had no problem walking right through them. Although I knew certain things were wrong because of the seed of Christ's Word that was planted within me as a young child, I chose to satisfy the desires that were awakened in my flesh.

After losing my virginity at only 14 years old, my self esteem along with my soul began to plummet into what seemed like a never-ending abyss. My "first-time" was not the fireworks I'd expected. I'm sure many of you can relate. In fact it was a nightmare. The day after I lost my virginity I found out my "boyfriend" was cheating on me. *Go figure!* A week after I lost my virginity, I noticed something was different as I began to itch! The young man had given me Crabs! And not the kind you buy from a seafood place! LOL So here I was –14 years old, just lost my virginity, and now with a STD. Although I thanked God it was something curable, I cried for weeks as any young girl would. I was completely heartbroken and without having a relationship with God at this point, I allowed myself to believe the negative voices in my head. "You aren't pretty enough; you're nasty; who really wants you; you aren't clean anymore; all men are dogs; they don't care about you so why should you care about them, etc. etc." This was the beginning of my "crying" stage. I cried a lot. No one knew it, but I was falling into a deep depression stemming from the low self-esteem I was allowing myself to have. It didn't help that I had horrible acne and I was a part of what the boys called the "Itty Bitty Titty Committee." My mother noticed I was always sad, and hated my sad demeanor. I'm sure it broke her heart as she consistently told me I was beautiful, but I didn't believe her. Instead I sought the approval from anyone who would pay attention.

Some would have thought that having that bad experience of losing my virginity would have scared me straight, right? Well instilling fear is not a long term solution to any problem! Love is the solution that is sustainable! I John 4:8 teaches us that God is love! Receiving a revelation of God's love for us is the only solution to any problem we face. However, it would be a long time before I received that understanding.

As my body developed as a teen and I began to discover the attention I received from wearing things that showed my shape, I began to purchase clothes that did just that. To make up for my "small" breasts, I accentuated my big butt! Looking back on it I can't believe I would wear leggings and a short shirt! I had no business dressing that way with all that "junk in the trunk!" Nonetheless, I loved the attention I was receiving. Promiscuous behaviors partnered with the way I was dressing. My pastors currently teach us to dress the way we would like to be addressed. On the flip side, back then I dressed as a "freak" because I wanted to be addressed as a "freak." During these teen years I felt as if I lost complete control of my flesh and little did I know, it I began to die.

*Romans 6:23, "For the wages which sin pays is death, but the [bountiful] free gift of God is eternal life through (in union with) Jesus Christ our Lord." **(Amplified Version)***

My heart also began to harden. Some men didn't understand how I was able to have sex with them and completely detach myself emotionally. After that first horrible experience being with a man, I built walls around my heart that would ultimately take years of work to tear down. Although a hard exterior began to develop, I was still a little innocent girl who loved and wanted to be loved by people, and was crying on the inside for that love. This female "pimpish" mentality carried over into relationships with women.

At 16 years old I was "turned out" by an older woman. "Turned out" was the term for Lesbians having sex with a straight woman and then turning them "gay." Or, as some may believe, this act of being "turned out" was unleashing or awakening a desire that was already within you. I can admit, I never truly had an inner desire for women. Only after surrounding myself with lesbians did that desire began to develop. Soon after that experience I began to meet women off of various chat rooms such as AOL and Black Planet, both popular social networks at the time. Meeting these women and building relationships and friendships with them cultivated this desire of being accepted and wanted. My esteem by this point was so low, that the idea of having women (whom I didn't believe could hurt me) in my corner that considered me "family" gave me a sense of security I hadn't had before. Deep down inside, locked away in my heart, were desires that I wouldn't admit were there.

I once dated and lived with an older woman who spoke of "commitment" ceremonies, and having children. No matter what I tried to tell myself and how I tried to fool myself, the idea of marrying this woman or having children with her just didn't seem right to me. I knew that I still wanted the big house with a white picket fence that was often symbolic of the "American Dream." Yet I wanted this dream with a "husband" and children who were all God-Fearing. I just didn't think or believe it was possible for me. Besides, look at all of the negative things I had went through and done.

Six years after I lost my virginity, I also had an abortion, abused marijuana and ecstasy, sold ecstasy, abused alcohol, shoplifted, engaged in several homosexual relationships and even attempted so-called "exotic" dancing. How did this once shy bookworm girl, who graduated from Banneker "Academic" High School in Washington, DC, a member of the Biology club and Odyssey of the Mind, who loved to read, and was a scripture quoting little girl get to this place? Satan was performing some of his best work in my life and for a few years I allowed him to succeed. Notice I said "allowed." We have to understand that what you allow on earth, God allows; and what you bind on earth God binds,

"I will give you the keys of the kingdom of heaven; and whatever you bind (declare to be improper and unlawful) on earth must be what is already bound in heaven; and whatever you loose (declare lawful) on earth must be what is already loosed in heaven." (Matthew16:19, Amplified Bible)

Living this defeated lifestyle began to just get old. Have you ever felt like you were just tired of being tired? When you are truly "tired" of something, it should move you to explore trying something different or possibly being open to something else other than what you are doing. Well it was at that point in my life that some major turning points began to occur.

In 2001, my mother became a partner of Spirit of Faith Christian Center under the tutelage of Pastor's Michael and Deloris Freeman. In my household, life as we knew it began to transform. As she began to apply the Word of "faith" into *her* life, over time *my* life as I knew it began to change. In the beginning of this change, I absolutely loathed my mother. I began to blame her for every failed relationship in my life. I was crazy enough at the time to insist that she stop praying for me. I thought her prayers were the cause of my problems because she was "co-partnering" with Jesus to make me unhappy. Besides I thought I was complete in my partying, my lustful lifestyle and my relationships. Right?!? Well as upside-down as that sounds that is exactly how I thought before the gradual renewing of my mind began to take place.

Romans 12:2, "And be not conformed to this world: but be ye transformed by the renewing of your mind, that ye may prove what that is good, and acceptable and perfect will of God." (KJV)

As the prayers of my righteous mom began to manifest, I began to realize just how miserable I was. There was definitely a void, a hunger that the women, men, drugs, alcohol and partying could not satisfy. I needed something greater, something more and something everlasting.

In July 2004, my best-friend and I rededicated our lives to Christ at Dr. Dee Dee Freeman's Birthday party. Nonetheless, for me, change did not come overnight and would not come without persistent obedience to God's Word. At that time, I was still living in a lesbian relationship. Labor Day weekend 2004, I had just returned home from partying in Atlanta for *Gay Pride*. Soon after arriving home, I received a phone call that would change my life forever. The best friend that was with me at Dr. Dee Dee's birthday party had been a victim of a drive-by shooting and was brain dead. She passed away on September 6, 2004. I never felt so much grief, pain and loss. We were like sisters. I was devastated and there was absolutely nothing that the woman I was in a relationship with could do about it. This woman took me to the Bahamas, bought me things and attempted to show me love the best way she knew how. Yet, there was still a void and now that my best friend had passed away, I recognized that void more than ever. On the other hand, there were times when I felt peace. These times were either at my church (Spirit of Faith Christian Center) or at my parent's house. It was there where I continually received the love of God. It was at those places where I knew no void.

November 2004, I made the decision to begin taking steps to leave a lifestyle I knew in my heart was contrary to the Word of God. I humbled myself and moved out of the house and like the Prodigal Son, I returned home. To humble myself meant I had to let go of the pride which prevented me from admitting that the lifestyle I was living most of my life was wrong. I thank God for loving parents who like our Father God, welcomed me back with open arms of love.

I will not deceive you by saying that once I moved back home that all of the sinful desires I had immediately disappeared. No, I still had sexual struggles with both men and women, which led me to backslide three times after I made the decision to return home. It was like I was on a see-saw of sin, but unlike the playground of my childhood this was not fun. Because I was now saved and sinning I was even more miserable than before. Day after day I felt nothing but guilt and condemnation for my unholy, unnatural, sexual desires. Note that I am not just speaking of sexual relations with women but sex with men outside of marriage as well. Finally, I prayed to God using these exact words like I was speaking to a friend, (I did not use any "thees, thous, shalls, or shall nots).

"Look I know you say in your Word that these things are an abomination unto you...Well, God it doesn't feel like it to me when I'm actually doing it...So, God I need to feel how you feel. Make me feel how you feel about it. I want to know what you feel, so I may forever please you!"

The next couple of weeks I was tested in the area of keeping my sexual purity with both men and women. It was to my surprise that I felt disgusted and detested each time. I was truly feeling how God feels as it relates to our sins. That's when I knew I was beginning to experience the manifestation of every prayer prayed in regards to my life.

I must make it clear that during this time of prayer manifestation, there was a course of obedience to God's Word that I had to follow. Being in tune to the voice of Holy Spirit by being immersed in His Word assisted me in transforming into the woman I am today. This did not come without struggle, yet my persistence to obey God paid off and each day life became easier. Finally submitting myself to the Will of God, I experienced the presence of God. In His presence I found out that there is a fullness of joy.

Psalm 16:11, "Thou will show me the path of life: in thy presence is fullness of joy; at thy right hand there are pleasures for evermore."

And in Christ I also found peace. In the midst of trouble I was finally able to maintain control and make wisdom guided decisions for my life. My old friends couldn't understand how I just didn't "trip" anymore and why I was always so happy.

Philippians 4:7, "And the peace of God, which passes all understanding, shall keep your hearts and minds through Christ Jesus."

That peace was familiar. It was the peace from my early childhood when I did not have a care in the world. Like Paul, I became a new creature!

2 Corinthians 5:17, "Therefore if any man be in Christ, he is a new creature: old things are passed away; behold all things are become new."

The old things and the ways of my flesh were no more and I became the new joyous, Spirit-filled, loving woman I am today. To God be the Glory! The Bible tells us in Acts 10:34 that God is no respecter of persons. This means that the same peace, the same joy, the same exciting, drama-free lifestyle is available for you, too.

You must understand that this is a gradual process, so don't become frustrated. Your persistence and determination to overcome is the key! The enemy wants you to become frustrated. He wants you to give up and return to your old ways. Don't give him the satisfaction of having any more victories in your life and begin to work the process. It is going to take perseverance, dedication, studying the Word of God, and prayer, which is communion with the Holy Spirit. Over the past few years, my life has done a 180 degree change and I am happier than I've ever been. I yearn to see others experience that same joy and peace that is eternal when you are in Jesus Christ and walking in His ways.

Dried Tears is my love offering to the Body of Christ. It is my love offering to you! I am a walking example that Jesus can and will pull you out of sexual perversion, drugs, greed, and anything else that is not of or like Him! Nothing is too hard for our God. He's just waiting on you to submit!

James 4:7, "Submit yourselves therefore to God. Resist the devil, and he will flee from you."
In this book you will find tools to assist you in drying the tears in your life. In other words, you will find tools that will release you from any pain you've experienced to live a life of peace! We all have a different story. You may not have had to endure anything traumatic, but that doesn't mean you haven't cried from experiencing or feeling some kind of emotional pain. Whether your life resembles a soap opera, or you are overcoming low self-esteem, a toxic relationship, a domestic violence situation, an eating disorder, drugs, etc. this book is for you! I am not a doctor, a psychiatrist, or a psychologist! As a matter of fact I am not

telling you to stop taking your medicine if a doctor prescribed it for depression or anything else. This book is simply to share wisdom that I've gained from having overcome various obstacles in my life. The Bible says in Revelation 12:11 that we overcome by the blood of the lamb and the words of our testimony! It is my heart's desire to see everyone walk in the fullness of life that God has already provided for us! Today I am a licensed minister and I own my own business called Unleashing Potential. My life's mission is to empower women and push them to their next level in life by encouraging them to be "Overcomers" and walk in purpose. I have been walking in sexual purity for several years, I no longer abuse drugs, nor am I depressed! I share these things with you not to brag but so that you can know the fruit behind what I am sharing. This book consists of various devotionals I have written from my study time that I pray will inspire you. The information in each chapter, along with the prayers, and journal exercises are designed to assist you in the path of becoming an "Overcomer!"

Now say this aloud with me |

"I am an Overcomer in All things!
God has given me the Power to Overcome any negative situation!
I walk in Power and Authority because He has given it to me!
I will Not Lose! I am a winner who has been named Victorious in all
things!"

You may be wondering why I had you say this out loud. Well one of the steps to being an "Overcomer" is that you have to start speaking like one! No more of this "woe is me" language. Proverbs 18:21 tells us that, "Death and Life are in the power of our tongue..." So as you read through this book, read aloud to yourself the various scriptures. Begin to practice speaking life to yourself! Alright Overcomer! Let's Go!

Chapter 1

Stop Right Here!

That if you confess with your mouth, "Jesus is Lord," and believe in your heart that God raised him from the dead, you will be saved. For it is with your heart that you believe and are justified, and it is with your mouth that you confess and are saved. (Romans 10:9-10, NIV)

First things first! We can talk about being an "Overcomer" all day, but if this matter of business is not taken care of, then the things I am about to share with you in the upcoming chapters won't have as much understanding and power. If you haven't yet done so, I want to invite you to enter into a personal relationship with Jesus Christ! You may be like I was once upon a time, thinking, "Oh no, this must mean I can't do this, and I can't do that! Or, I'm young and having fun, I'll do it when I'm older." Well please believe this, you may not be able to do it when you get older because tomorrow isn't promised! Now this isn't an attempt to scare you into a relationship with God, but an opportunity to bless you and change your life forever!

I used to think a life without Christ was more fun! Boy was I sadly mistaken! I once thought that if I'd accept Christ I would have to lose all of my flavor, and style. I was to become this boring person who just listened to choirs all day, quoted scripture, and wore no makeup and long skirts. Absolutely NOT! This is not what being a Christian is about!

Being a Christian is about having a relationship with Jesus Christ, God's son, who was sent down to save us from our sins. If you read Genesis 2 you will see the fall of man (Adam) and from that point on, men and women needed a savior. Without the savior, we are lost in this world! So how is Jesus our savior? Well do you remember those old Nextel phones? They possessed a feature called, "direct connect." This feature allowed you to push a button and directly connect with the person you have the direct connect with, enabling you to have clear communication. Well Jesus is the Christian's "direct connect." He is our "direct connect" to our Heavenly Father. With him, our sins are covered by His blood and now our Father clearly hears us. Acts 4:12 tells us that, *"Salvation is found in no one else, for there is no other name under heaven given to men by which we must be saved."* *(NIV)*

By asking Christ into our hearts we not only have the direct connect to the Father, we have a friend who will be closer to you than a brother! With this friend in your life, you are an "Overcomer!" So if you haven't officially received salvation, feel free to pray the prayer below! Congratulations in advance on taking this exciting step in your freedom! Your life will never be the same!

Prayer | *Father in the name of Jesus, I confess that I am a sinner in need of a Savior. I repent of all of my sins and ask that you come into my heart. I believe your son died on the Cross and rose on the third day so that I may be saved. I receive your salvation on this day and choose to follow you! In Jesus name, Amen!*

Journal Exercise | ☺

Write down this date and memorialize it! This is your new birth date because if you've prayed that prayer, you have been now born again as a new creature in Christ! Read II Corinthians 5:17 and write the verse out next to your new birth date! This will serve as a reminder of your new life! Now go out and celebrate! Have some cake! Why? Because now you have two birthdays!

_____

_____

_____

Chapter 2

What About Your Friends?

*II Corinthians 6:17-18-"So, come out from among
[unbelievers], and separate (sever) yourselves from them,
says the Lord, and touch not [any] unclean thing; then I will
receive you kindly and treat you with favor,18And I will be
a Father to you, and you shall be My sons and daughters,
says the Lord Almighty." (Amplified Version)*

Today is a new day! Now that you have
acknowledged and confessed Jesus Christ as Lord and you
believe in your heart that God has raised him from the dead
you are saved! (Romans 10:9-10) Jesus bore your sins on
the cross and now you are in right standing with him. He
forgives you, and loves you, and remembers your sins no
more! But now you are probably wondering, "What's next?"
Or, "Why haven't these ungodly feelings gone away?" You
may still feel the urge to call up Mr. or Miss "So and So." You
may still want to pick up a drink, a cigarette, a blunt! You
may still "feel" as though nothing has changed! Do not be
alarmed. You will learn that Overcomers live by faith and
not how they feel!

No matter what temptations you experience, God has provided a way of escape in his word. By obeying his Word, you are bringing forth fruit (evidence), consistent with your repentance (changed heart). (Luke 3:7-8) Let me give it to you straight. Now that you've decided to live for Christ, you will have challenges in your walk.   Although angels in heaven are rejoicing, Satan and his "little" helpers are enraged. He wants to take out the Word that was sown in your heart.

Mark 4:15 -"And these are they by the way side, where the Word is sown; but when they have heard, Satan cometh immediately, and taketh away the Word that was sown in their hearts." (KJV)

When I first accepted Christ I was still living in a sexually perverse relationship; thus being outside of God's perfect will for my life. I was so excited about the change I knew had taken place inside of me. I told the "woman" I was seeing and my "friends" at the time about my experience. Immediately, I was chastised and made fun of. I received comments like, "*Oh.. so what... now you are going to mess with men and become a gay basher?*" That was the furthest thing from my mind at that time; I was just excited that I had received Christ. However, because I did not "come out from among them, and separate myself," their comments began to affect me. I thought that although I was making a decision to change my life that I could still have the same friends and associates. How wrong was I? As soon as I received Christ I returned to my same environment not giving the word an opportunity to take root. It was as if a crack addict became free from smoking crack but still wanted to hang out with friends in the

I thought that although I was making a decision to change my life that I could still have the same friends and associates. How wrong was I?

crack house! It's as if someone decides to stop tricking but still wants to be around prostitutes or her former pimp. It's nearly impossible to walk in freedom and still be closely tied to those in bondage! This was a very critical time in my development because I was a baby in Christ and still easily influenced by my friends at the time. Needless to say, I didn't go back to church to rededicate my life to God until three years later...

The decision you've just made to live for Christ and to be an Overcomer is one to be taken seriously. In order to begin to successfully walk in your deliverance, you must separate yourself from unbelievers. The bible tells us *in **II***

Corinthians 6:14-15:

"Do not be unequally yoked with unbelievers [do not make mismatched alliances with them or come under a different yoke with them, inconsistent with your faith]. For what partnership have right living and right standing with God with iniquity and lawlessness? Or how can light have fellowship with darkness? What harmony can there be between Christ and Belial [the devil]? Or what has a believer in common with an unbeliever?" (Amplified)

I love the way the message bible puts it.

"Don't become partners with those who reject God. How can you make a partnership out of right and wrong? That's not partnership; that's war. Is light best friends with dark? Does Christ go strolling with the Devil? Do trust and mistrust hold hands?" (Message)

Continuing your friendships and your relationships with those who commit the sins you are delivered from is like Christ walking through the park, hanging out with the Devil. As crazy as that may look, that's how crazy you must look to God when you continue to hold on to your past relationships with unbelievers. Note that unbelievers in this case are not just limited to those who don't know Christ. This goes for those who aren't making an attempt to strive for the things of God. For example, after you have made the decision to walk in your freedom that is in Christ, and to stop the fornication, it's not okay to continue to hang out with your "church-friend" who is still choosing to fornicate. So what she "goes to church?" You are still unequally yoked! Come out from among him/her and separate yourself! This may seem extreme at first. Yet take comfort in knowing that whatever God asks you to leave alone, he replaces it with something greater, more profitable, and you will have peace in having it. You may hear, "Who does she think she is? Does she think she's better than us? She's now too good for us? Blah, Blah, Blah!" I heard all of the above! Yet at that point I had to be like, "What about your friends?"...If they could not support and respect my decision to do something to make my life better, then are they really friends to begin with? Selah. (Think on that!)...

When I separated myself from people who did not want to live for God, he replaced those individuals with people of like interests who had the same spirit of faith! Today, I have true friendships and relationships with people who are in Christ.

God has your best interests in mind by commanding us to be separate and to not walk together with unbelievers.

My pastor Dr. Michael Freeman puts it this way, "Get away from those who have your problems and get with those who have your answer!" A friend who is still trying to keep you in the same place and not help you to grow obviously does not have your answer. Position yourself to experience all of the awesome things that are available from obeying His Word; and aligning yourself with those who don't have your problems!

Prayer | Father in the name of Jesus, I thank you for delivering me from _____(enter challenges here). I thank you for sending your son Jesus to die on the cross for those sins and for giving me the opportunity to be free. Father, I thank you for exposing, revealing, and removing all of those people that do not have my best interest at heart. I thank you for sending people in my life that will provoke me unto love and good works. I thank you for being strength at this my time. I believe I receive these things by faith! Lord have your way in my life! In Jesus' name I pray Amen!

Journal Exercise | ☺

Write down and pray about the names of the people you need to separate yourself from? Ask God to reveal those who are holding you back from any progress you are having in Christ. Use the journal to create a list and hold yourself accountable to that list. Write down any necessary steps you may need to take in order to do just that. Examples: change your phone number, stop hanging out at the local bowling alley where all of your old friends are. Now that you've written these things down, seek God on how to go about taking action!

Names |

_____

_____

_____

_____

_____

Steps |

_____

_____

_____

_____

_____

_____

_____

_____

_____

_____

_____

_____

_____

Chapter 3

Controlling Your Thoughts

2 Corinthians 10:5, "Casting down imaginations, and every high thing that exalteth itself against the knowledge of God, and bringing into captivity every thought to the obedience of Christ." (KJV)

During this process more than likely you will experience all types of thoughts contrary to the word of God. Some of them may sound like this, "You'll never be delivered! You'll never be good enough! God will never forget *your* sins; you've done too much dirt!" Well I have news for you: it's all a lie from the pit of hell! I once had a "thought" problem! Sometimes I still do, and I have to do as 2 Corinthians 10:5 says and cast that thought down.

When I first rededicated my life to Christ, I was attending a class at my church called Disciples of Christ. Although I was now serious about God, I didn't have any friends because I had separated from the ones I did have that were still living how I used to live. I wanted to be social; I just acted shy at the time. So after this class at church a girl approached me and she began to compliment my shoes. Now that got my attention, because ladies how many of you know we enjoy compliments! Well then this girl asked me was I from Louisiana? You would have thought I saw a ghost! Now this may seem like a normal question to some. But automatically I allowed my thoughts

How many opportunities do we miss out on because of our refusal to take charge over dumb, negative, thoughts!

to take me down a negative road! "Who does she think she is? Does she think I'm country? I'm from D.C.!" Now note, those of you who read this book who aren't from Washington, DC may not see where the issue was. However, Washingtonians are very passionate about where they are from and some can be insulted if you even think they are from somewhere else! LOL. Little did I know she only asked me that question because she was from Louisiana and I reminded her of home! This girl asking me that question was actually a compliment! Well after I told the girl I was from D.C., we still exchanged numbers and today she is one of my best-friends! She was a person God sent me who had my answer!

And guess what? Because of my negative thoughts, I could have almost missed a divine connection in my life! How many opportunities do we miss out on because of our refusal to take charge over dumb, negative, thoughts!

When a thought comes into your mind and you are not sure what its origin is, there are 3 steps that need to be taken.

1. The first step is to quickly **_locate it_**. Pray and ask God where is this thought coming from? An easy barometer for measuring whether or not the thought is from God is to ask yourself these questions. Is this something I can find in the Bible? Does this thought line up with the word of God, thus being given by the Holy Spirit our helper who leads and guides us into all truth? Is my soul conjuring up these thoughts? (Example: thoughts of insecurity or bitterness from past hurts) Or, is this thought in direct contrast with what God said in his word? (Example: thoughts of immorality, going back to an unrighteous lifestyle and/or way of living).

2. Once you've located the particular thought the next step is to **_take action_**. If this is a thought that lines up with the word of God, great! That means the Holy

Spirit is just loving up on you and sharing His heart for you. However, if this is a thought that does not come from God, that's when the "casting down" method of 2 Corinthians 10:5 becomes necessary. Let me give you an example. After my deliverance from sexual perversion I was plagued with sexual dreams at times with men and at times with women. I knew that those dreams did not come from God. For awhile I continued to have them until I learned this principal of "casting down." I began to find scriptures that talked about not fulfilling the lusts of the flesh and personalized them for myself. Then I would confess these scriptures on a daily basis. *Example: (I live in the spirit; therefore I walk in the spirit not fulfilling the lusts of the flesh. I present my body as a living sacrifice, holy and acceptable which is my reasonable service. I cast down imaginations and every high thing that exalts itself against the knowledge of God. I bring my thoughts into captivity to the obedience of Christ. [Galatians 5:18, Romans 12:1; 2 Corinthians 10:5])* The way to cast down ungodly thoughts, which are against the knowledge of God, is to replace them with Godly thoughts that are in line with the knowledge of God. We find the knowledge of God in the Word of God i.e. the Bible. The "Word of God is quick, and powerful, and sharper than any two-edged sword." (Hebrews 4:12) So picture this...Every time the enemy comes at you with a thought, you respond by coming at him with a two edge sword literally knocking him off his rocker every time.

3. Now that you've located scripture references, personalized them, and began to confess them over your situation, the third step is to **_meditate_**. Webster's New World Dictionary defines meditate as, "to think deeply." The Hebrew word for meditate is, "Hagah" which means to ponder and to mutter. When I am meditating on the word of God, I am speaking my confessions over and over again in a low indistinct tone. Notice I said a "low indistinct tone." Meditating on the word does not have to be spooky. If you begin walking around on your job loudly saying, "I walk in the spirit and I don't fulfill the lusts of the flesh!" Don't be surprised when your supervisor calls you into his office to reprimand you and don't be surprised when you are known as the

"crazy Christian." Do not mistake foolishness for zeal! As you begin to meditate regularly it will become second nature for you to use the Word to bring your thoughts into the obedience of Christ.

DO NOT mistake foolishness for zeal!

Meditating on the Word will not only empower you to control your thought life, but give you the ability to be successful in all areas of your Christian life. Joshua 1:8 says, "This Book of the Law shall not depart from your mouth, but you shall meditate in it day and night, that you may observe to do according to all that is written in it. For then you will make your way prosperous, and then you will have good success." (NKJV) The person who has good success and has made their way prosperous meditates on the word on a very regular and consistent basis. Joshua says, "day and night" not "on Sunday's when I go to church." When we meditate on the word of God we are speaking God's best into our lives. The Bible is not just a book of, "thou shalts" and "thou shalt nots." It is a book that contains the benefit package or the perfect will for your life. This is a principle that is still very active in my life. Just because I have been walking in deliverance for years does not mean that this practice of casting down imaginations is not still being utilized. Even during the writing of this book I have had to cast down imaginations of failure, and fear. However, I use the same principles I'm sharing here and I train my mind to think on what's right according to Philippians 4:8,

"Finally, my friends, keep your minds on whatever is true, pure, right, holy, friendly, and proper. Don't ever stop thinking about what is truly worthwhile and worthy of praise." (CEV)

Putting this principal into action will give you authority over your thoughts, ultimately revolutionizing your Christian walk.

Journal Exercise | ☺

Prayer | Father in the name of Jesus, I thank you for being Lord over my life. Because you are Lord over my life, I make you Lord over my thoughts. Your Word says that your blood purifies my conscience from any dead works. Therefore, because of your bloodshed on the cross my conscience is pure, my thoughts are pure. (Hebrews 9:14) I take authority over thoughts that are not of you and I bring them to the obedience of your Word. My mind is surrendered to you. In Jesus' name I pray, Amen.

*What types of thoughts are you thinking? A famous line from the movie, "Eat, Pray, Love" came to mind when writing this chapter: "You have to learn to select your thoughts, the same way that you select your clothes everyday." Use resources such as **www.biblegateway.com**, and **www.crosswalk.com** to locate scriptures that reference your particular situation, and begin to meditate on them. These websites have search engines that allow you to input keywords such as "fear," "obedience," "lust" etc. Then the site will list every scripture in the bible that uses that particular word. After you've located scriptures pertaining to your situation, begin to turn them into personal confessions as I did in step number two **action.** Lastly, after you've completed these steps use this page in your journal as a reference for mediating on your confessions.*

_____
_____
_____
_____
_____
_____
_____
_____
_____
_____
_____
_____

Chapter 4

I Can't Believe They Did This to Me!

The enemy hunted me down; he kicked me and stomped me within an inch of my life. He put me in a black hole, buried me like a corpse in that dungeon. I sat there in despair, my spirit draining away, my heart heavy, like lead. (Psalm 143:3-4, Message Translation)

Pretty dramatic huh? In this verse David sounds like he is in a lot of pain and darkness. The truth is, many of us are living like David lived in this particular passage of scripture. We have been cheated on, lied too, abused, misused, abandoned, violated; this list can go on and on! It doesn't take an intelligent person to know that this is true. Look around you! People are hurting all over. Some drown themselves in drugs or alcohol because this is how they choose to deal with the pain. Personally that was one of the ways I coped, or should I say attempted to cope with pain. Anytime I was hurt, I would have a drink or smoke a "J." For those that don't know, smoking a "J" is a Washington, D.C. phrase for smoking a blunt or smoking weed. In 2000 I was introduced to XTC pills. These pills would produce a false sense of happiness. Yet at the end of the high, you would feel worse than before because it was no true solution to the pain. Others self mutilate or cut themselves. Some turn to sex or entertain abusive partners. All of these ways that people tend to deal with pain have the potential to be detrimental. In fact, they simply act as a Bandaid and not a solution. Just as a Bandaid covers a scar, we may do destructive things to cover up pain.

The dangerous thing about pain is this: if it's not dealt with it will manifest itself through ways that are not only dangerous to our health but our souls. Pain will hinder your prosperity! 3 John 1:2 states,

"Dear friend, I pray that you may enjoy good health and that all may go well with you, even as your soul is getting along well." (NIV)

But I submit to you that your soul and health will be directly affected if we allow ourselves to wallow in hurt. As you've read in my personal story, I have had to overcome various painful situations and circumstances in life. From being cheated on, to being lied too, to being taken advantage of, from being betrayed; yep, there was a reason I once cried a lot! I have been hurt more times than I can count. Many times, these things were done by the people closest to me. As you may relate, this tends to hurt the most. Yet, what are we to do? Stay mad? Hurt? Avoid those individuals who have hurt us?

I once avoided those who hurt me. It was such an inconvenience! I would miss out on family cookouts or friend's events just because I refused to go in the atmosphere of someone who hurt me. I would do these things all because I didn't want to face the issue or I was still wallowing in hurt! Ultimately, these actions were rooted in fear and not in love because; perfect love (which is the Love of God) casts out fear." Let's look at this verse verbatim,

...people are not perfect. Only God is perfect. Therefore people are capable of hurting you. It's what we choose to do with the pain that will take us from hurt to healing!

"There is no fear in love. But perfect love drives out fear, because fear has to do with punishment. The one who fears is not made perfect in love." (I John 4:18, NIV)

Living this way was causing me to live a miserable life. At the end of the day, we must understand that people are not perfect. Only God is perfect. Therefore people are capable of hurting you. It's what we choose to do with the pain that will take us from hurt to healing!

I'm going to share with you three things that helped me to overcome all of the hurt and pain I've experienced in life. I used to believe that the fact that this pain was gone was some supernatural miracle from God. Then I realized that this wasn't a miracle; I had just committed myself to doing things from His word no matter how it felt. God has already given us the answers in His word. God is not a magician! He's our Father, our Friend, The Almighty, who has given us the keys and the ability to Overcome! So now let's unlock this thing so you can get over the hurt!

Key Points | To Overcome Hurt

The first key point is this: in order to overcome hurt, you have to overcome self. Your "self" wants to be led by its emotions. Your emotions will keep you frustrated, crying, upset, and mad if you allow them too. Overcoming hurt means you must gain control of these emotions. "Self" has to use self control over the emotions in order to ultimately Forgive! Yes Forgive! It's not a dirty word although it can feel like a dirty job! We all must do it at some point or another! But why? I am not saying emotions are a bad thing! God has given each of us emotions. Crying, sometimes screaming helps us to release pain and anger. However, crying and screaming does not have the power to heal our pain! That is why ultimately gaining control over our emotions and forgiving is so critical to the healing process. Why do I have to forgive the one who violated me as a child? Why do I have to forgive the one who raped me, lied on me, cheated, etc.?

Now don't become apprehensive because forgiveness doesn't mean you must become great friends with this individual and live happily ever after with them. Forgiveness is not even about them! You forgive for YOU! Most of the time when we hold on to that thing which the person has done to hurt us, they have moved on with their lives. They may not even be thinking about you! Yet here we are mad, hurt, and disgusted. Forgiveness allows us to release that pain and move on.

Not only must we forgive because of the benefit of releasing that pain; we "forgive" because we are of the "forgiven" who will always need "forgiveness!" Matthew 6:15 says, *"But if you do not forgive men their sins, your*

Father will not forgive your sins." You may wonder, "Well they keep hurting me, keep disappointing me, how many times should I forgive?" You and one of Jesus' disciples Peter had the same question. *"Then Peter came to Jesus and asked, "Lord, how many times shall I forgive my brother or sister who sins against me? Up to seven times?" Jesus answered, "I tell you, not seven times, but seventy-seven times." (Matthew 18:21-22, NIV)* This is because our willingness to forgive should never end! Is God asking you to trust this same individual who continues to hurt you? No, that's not wisdom. Nonetheless, forgiveness is for OUR health because no one is worth you carrying pain. This verse helped me to walk out the forgiving process that was ultimately hindering the healing process.

Ephesians 6:12 (Amplified Bible)-For we are not wrestling with flesh and blood [contending only with physical opponents], but against the despotisms, against the powers, against [the master spirits who are] the world rulers of this present darkness, against the spirit forces of wickedness in the heavenly (supernatural) sphere.

So what does this verse means? It brings me to the second thing that will help you to "Overcome" the hurt once you understand. We must realize that it is the enemy (Satan and his demonic helpers) that's spoken about in Ephesians 6:12 (*physical opponents, master of spirits, world ruler of present darkness, forces of wickedness*) who influences and works through people to hurt us. What does this mean? It means that we are to direct any anger toward the evil one who is Satan. He is the influencer behind the destruction of families, the inventor of molestation, rape, and other perverse acts. This verse tells us that our fight isn't against something or someone physical, but in the supernatural. So we can't overcome hurt through and by physical measures because our fight is not physical. This is why when we attempt to argue, scream, cry, drink or party our pain away, it only feels good for a moment. Yet it never fails that the pain will revisit you because you attempted to relieve the pain through physical measures. When someone does something to upset or hurt me, I have learned to get mad at the enemy (the evil influencer) because I know that the person is being used by him.

Lastly, stop pressing the rewind button in your mind! Our mind wants to replay bad experiences like it's your favorite song! You continue to download negative experience after experience every time you rewind or replay the event in your mind! Now that you are committing to take charge of your emotions, and forgive the individual(s) who've hurt you, now it's time to simply release them and the situation to God. We cannot effectively do that if we allow ourselves to press rewind. God has given us the power to forgive! Today, let's commit to walk in it and not allow that bad situation to hurt us any longer!

Prayer | *Father, I thank you for sending your son Jesus to die for me so that I can be forgiven. As you have forgiven me, Father I forgive those (say name of person here) who have hurt me. Lord you were chastised for my peace (Isaiah 53:5) and so I cast my cares and burdens on you; the one who cares for me. Lord, continue to guide me on this love walk, in Jesus' Name, Amen!*

Journal Exercise | ☺

Get a large sheet or sheets of paper. Write down the names of anyone or any situation that you can think of that has caused or may be currently causing you any hurt or pain. Write down those same names in this journal. Lastly, on the sheet of paper where you've written their names and the situation that has caused you pain; I want you to tear it up and throw it away! This symbolizes your release of the situation! If you've prayed the prayer in this chapter, this means you've prayed for those who've hurt you! The fact that you prayed for them is what I call "Big Girl Stuff!" Overcomers, do the "Big Girl Stuff!"

Names

Chapter 5

The Awakening – Is It Your Season to Love?

I charge you, O daughters all over the world,
By the gazelles or by the does of the field,
Do not stir up nor awaken love
Until it pleases

{The Prelude}

Yeah, yeah, I hear that
But he's fine though
Butter pecan complexion
Over 6 feet
And his smile makes me weak
So to speak
I am enjoying our conversations
As we are gradually graduating
To deeper and more intimate topics
About our favorite movies to
What we went through as a child
To our past mistakes
And things we did worthwhile
Up on the phone until 2 AM
God I am loving this man…

"I charge you, O daughters all over the world,
By the gazelles or by the does of the field,
Do not stir up nor awaken love
Until it pleases"

{The Climax}

And get this…I love being in his arms
In the calm, cool, breeze
Everything seems so serene
So right for now
And prayerfully forever
He's just for me
I know to be careful
And of course I won't fornicate
I can trust myself
To be at his house
Very, very, late
Besides I'm grown
I can handle these dates
Alone…

"I charge you, O daughters all over the world,
By the gazelles or by the does of the field,
Do not stir up nor awaken love
Until it pleases"

{The After Effect}

Longing to touch him
Kiss him, Hug him
And more
Am I playing myself?
By opening these doors
Preludes to covenant behavior
But I'm not there
I used to say I'd never put my lips on
Or touch a man
That was not my husband

And now I'm going there?
How did I get here?
I say I love Christ
But does my body love him too?
We want to trust ourselves
And our flesh
So for that… we played the fool
No rules, no boundaries
Going with the flow
My body is telling me yes
Yet my mind is telling me no
All because I chose
Not to listen to the charge
Don't stir up or awaken love
Until a covenant is established by far…

Please hear me…
"I charge you, O daughters all over the world,
By the gazelles or by the does of the field,
Do not stir up nor awaken love
Until it pleases…"

Excerpts taken from the Song of Solomon

I wrote this poem in 2007 when I was beginning to understand fully the importance of sexual purity during the process of being an "Overcomer." My past views of sex and relationships were deeply tainted and I had to renew my mind, specifically in this area. Although I was in a process of receiving emotional healing, I allowed myself to engage in relationships prematurely. Why do I say prematurely? Well, as Ecclesiastes 3:1 states, *"To everything there is a season, A time for every purpose under heaven…" (NKJV)* So if there is a season to everything, and a time for every purpose, then I submit to you that there is a season for you to be in a romantic relationship. Now this particular statement does not apply to my married ladies because if you are already married, you must use the principles in the Word of God to keep your marriage healthy!

Everyday another woman delays her destiny by stepping out in a romantic relationship during the wrong season.

God created us to be emotional beings. However, He's also given us the ability and the power to control our emotions. I like how the Message Bible puts Ecclesiastes 3:1. It says, *"There is an opportune time to do things; a right time for everything on earth."* There will be an appointed time in our lives when we are able to express ourselves freely with our husbands. Understand this, the "Overcomer" is not moved by her emotions and vulnerabilities! This is when Satan likes to attack the most; when we are feeling vulnerable or needy. This is when he may send Mr. Oh So Fine, who says all the right lines, while he wines and dines you, right to the day your panties come off! Yes it may sound extreme to some, but this is happening everyday! Everyday another woman delays her destiny by stepping out in a romantic relationship during the wrong season. Am I anti-relationship? Absolutely not! We were created to desire and enjoy God ordained, equally yoked companionship. I am against making a decision that can negatively affect your destiny and overall purpose! I wrote the poem at the beginning of this chapter when I was ending a relationship. This relationship had challenges that mirrored those in the poem. Looking back on the situation, I realized that I had no business being in a relationship during that season of my life, period! This was a time where I should have been solely focused on the call that God has on my life, while developing a love relationship with Him. Yet in a moment of vulnerability and not properly guarding my heart, I entered into a romantic relationship before the proper time.

"Keep and guard your heart with all vigilance and above all that you guard, for out of it flow the springs of life."
(Proverbs 4:23, Amplified)

The relationship was a time of constant stress, strain, and struggle. Although we did not have sexual intercourse, we consistently played games of Russian roulette with our flesh. You may be thinking how did that happen, Miss Sexual Purity Worth the Wait Overcomer in Everything Guru?! It happened because I allowed myself to "awaken love before its proper time."

Understand something: you cannot trust your flesh! There is not one thing about it that you can trust. That's why God calls us to walk in the Spirit so that we will not fulfill the lusts of the flesh. Sure there are people who kiss and hug and never engage in the actual sexual act, but why play ourselves by getting all worked up just to stop?! I mean let's be real. There aren't many of us, including myself, who can engage in those acts and not desire to go all the way. Why?! These acts are called "foreplay."

The definition of foreplay | *Erotic stimulation preceding sexual intercourse 2: action or behavior that precedes an event.*

So if we are living a life or desiring to honor God with our bodies while we are single, engaging in foreplay is a direct contradiction. What is the point of engaging in a behavior that precedes an event I'm not even supposed to be attending until marriage? God loves us so-o-o much that he created this action called "foreplay" to prepare us to enjoy sex all the more with our husbands. Our bodies are designed to fully enjoy these actions within the confines of marriage. We aren't supposed to have to start and then stop! Speaking from experience, that makes things so-o-o much harder. You then have to step away, renew your mind, cast down imaginations, etc. etc. So I charge you ladies of the world! "Don't excite love, don't stir it up, until the time is ripe-and you're ready." (Song of Solomon 3:5, Message).

My pastor always teaches us to be "Season, System, Sensitive people." Be sensitive to the season you are in. Pray and ask God if it is O.K. for you to engage in a relationship at this very season of your life. "Overcomers" will save themselves a lot of tears if they do not awaken love before its time!

Prayer | *Father, I thank You for Your grace and mercy. I know that You have called me to a life of holiness, purity, and sanctification. This can only be accomplished by living a Spirit-led life. Therefore I walk in the Spirit and I do not fulfill the desires of the flesh. Holy Spirit have Your way in my life! Continue to lead me and guide me into all truth by opening my eyes to any compromising situations I may be in so that I can make the change. Give me the wisdom to know what season I am in and what I should be focusing on at this very moment in time. Expose, reveal and remove all of those that do not have my best interests at heart! In Jesus' name, Amen!*

Journal Exercise | ☺

Awareness is everything! We are each driven and can be awakened by our own lusts! What may excite me may not necessarily excite you! For example: Some people cannot hold hands without wanting to have sex! Some people cannot be out late with their significant other without wanting to have sex! However, some people can do these things without it having any effect on them at all. I encourage you to write down the particular things that seem to awaken your flesh. What are your triggers? Is it a certain type of music or movie? Is it being around a specific type of person? Identify an "accountability partner" to assist you in this area. An accountability partner is a parent, friend, and/or mentor that you allow to hold you accountable in the areas where you've had challenges. Show them this exercise and ask them to regularly check on you to see how you are doing in these areas. Being aware of your triggers helps you to identify when you are headed in a direction that can take you away from walking in God's Perfect Will for your life; which is holiness.

_____

_____

_____

_____

_____

_____

_____

_____

Chapter 6

Study + Meditation = Successful Overcomer!

II Timothy 2:15 - Study to show thyself approved unto God, a workman that needeth not to be ashamed, rightly dividing the word of truth.

Joshua 1:8 - This book of the law shall not depart out of thy mouth; but thou shall meditate therein day and night, that thou mayest observe to do according to all that is written therein: for then thou shalt make thy way prosperous, and then thou shalt have good success.

Psalm 1:2-3 - But his delight is in the law of the Lord; And in his law doth he meditate day and night. And he shall be like a tree planted by the rivers of water, that bringeth forth his fruit in his season. His leaf also shall not wither; And whatsoever he doeth shall prosper.

Acts 17:11- These were more noble than those in Thessalonica, in that they receive the word with all readiness of mind, and searched the scriptures daily, whether those things were so.
(King James Version)

Many times, when we hear the word "study," it brings about a certain unpleasant feeling. You remember the days you spent coming home from school being forced to study your English, math, history, etc., and you were told that studying all of these things, and increasing your knowledge, would get you to a successful place in life; being able to pay your bills and take care of your family.

Many of us were taught that we need to study so we can get into a good college, get a good job, and live the "good life." You will have a family with two children, a dog named, "Rover," a house with a white picket fence, and a nice car. That's typically what's considered the, "American Dream." It's the world's picture perfect idea of success. An individual who has these things appears as if they've "made it" to some degree. Nonetheless, behind the scenes they may be experiencing marital infidelity, unruly children, constant depression, low self-worth, workaholic tendencies, and/or the consistent disruption of peace. I submit to you that even with all of the "right" things in place, without knowledge of the Word of God, this family will not have "good" success according to God's Word. The "Overcomer's" success is due to their meditation and study of the Word of God, their application of that Word, and walking in their purpose!

Although certain rappers may define being successful as simply having "the money, cars, and clothes," please know that true success means so much more. My pastor, Dr. Michael Freeman defines understanding as, "Divine comprehension in my heart that gives me the ability to repeat something at will." When you understand the Word of God, you are able to repeat its precepts during the pressure times, such as temptation to walk in sexual immorality, when sickness attacks your body or your family, or not knowing where the money is going to come from to pay a particular bill.

Do I enjoy studying? I do, but I guess the "researcher" in me has always loved studying. I realize, though, that studying may be a challenge for some, especially when it comes to the Bible. The very first Bible translation that I used was a New International Version (NIV) Student Bible. In the beginning of my Christian walk, I simply could not get with the "thee's" "thous" "thys" and "shalts" of the King James Version Translation of the Bible. Do not be discouraged because you feel as though you don't understand what you are reading. Simply purchase a translation of the Bible that is easy for you to understand. As you grow in your basic understanding of the Bible, you will then feel more comfortable to move towards other translations. Today, I simply love reading and studying the

King James Version of the Bible. However, years ago I was simply okay with reading from the NIV, Message Translation, or even a Children's Bible! Whatever translation of the Bible is easier for you to understand, begin studying with that!

Understanding this Word is what keeps us bringing forth fruit in its season; prospering in everything we put our hands on, and walking in good health.

God wants to propel us to an area of abundance so that we can be blessed and be a blessing to others, thus exhibiting His love and glory to the world.

3 John 2 says,

"Dear friend, I pray that you may enjoy good health and that all may go well with you, even as your soul is getting along well." (NIV)

This is God's desire for his children. I love the way the Amplified Bible puts it,

"Now to Him Who, by (in consequence of) the [action of His] power that is at work within us, is able to [carry out His purpose and] do superabundantly, far over and above all that we [dare] ask or think [infinitely beyond our highest prayers, desires, thoughts, hopes, or dreams]. (Ephesians 3:20)

His desire for us is to live not just the "good life," but a "superabundant" life, in Him! God wants to propel us to an area of abundance so that we can be blessed and be a blessing to others, thus exhibiting His love and glory to the world. Joshua 1:8 says if we meditate on the Word of God, and work towards actually doing the Word in our lives, then we will make our way prosperous and have "good" success. Psalms 1:2-3 says that when we meditate on the Word day and night, that "whatsoever" we do shall prosper! Knowing this truth has literally revolutionized my life, helping me to be an "Overcomer" in all areas! Understanding how to apply God's Word gives us the ability to get along with people on our jobs, and have peaceful relationships with our family and friends. "Good" success and prosperity not only includes having the material things; it means that we are fruitful in all areas of our lives.

Now that we've discussed the importance of study and meditation, let's explore how to carry it out. The act of interpretation of a word, scripture, or passage, in the Bible is called exegesis. In order to properly 'exegete' scripture, there are some tools you will need to use. First, you will need a Bible dictionary. One that I recommend is the *Vine's Expository Dictionary of Old & New Testament Words*. This dictionary has the meaning of thousands of words in the Old and New Testaments in their original Hebrew and Greek texts. Secondly, you will need a Bible Concordance. A concordance is an alphabetical list of words in the Bible with references to the passages where they occur. One that I recommend is the *New Strong's Exhaustive Concordance of the Bible*. In this concordance, you can find every scripture in the Bible, as well as their original Hebrew and Greek meanings.

When interpreting the Word of God, it is also helpful to use commentaries. A commentary is simply a series of explanatory notes and remarks about a particular scripture or passage. Many Bibles come with commentaries inside of them. Some Bible commentaries I recommend are the *Scofield's Bible, Matthew Henry's Bible Commentary, Joyce Meyer's The Everyday Life Bible*, and *The Life Application Bible*. Commentaries are designed to assist in opening up the word to you. However, they are not to be the final authority in the interpretation process. We are living in an age of technology where we have the awesome advantage of accessing the information super highway - the internet. These websites not only have Bible commentaries, but you can view several translations of the Bible that may help you obtain a greater understanding of the Word during your study time.

- ～ www.biblegateway.com
- ～ www.blueletterbible.com
- ～ www.bible.com
- ～ www.crosswalk.com

You are now ready to have the success of an "Overcomer!"

———————————— ————————————

Prayer | *Father in the name of Jesus, I thank you for your Word. Create in me a clean heart and renew a right, steadfast spirit within me. Give me an increased desire to seek Your face daily, so that I may understand your Word, having "good" success in everything that I do. I thank you in advance for giving me divine revelation as I began to study to show myself approved. In Jesus' name I pray, Amen!*

Journal Exercise | ☺

Select a scripture or passage in the Bible and prayerfully meditate on it. Pray and ask God how you should apply that Word to your everyday life. Utilize some of the resources mentioned in this chapter in order to dig deeper as you "rightly divide the word of truth." (II Timothy 2:15) Share the Word you will apply with an accountability partner. Make a commitment to check with them in 30 days to see how you have done on applying the particular verse to your life.

Iron Sharpening Tip: A good way to meditate is to repeat the scripture softly to yourself over and over again.

Chapter 7

An Overcomer Activates Their Lifeline

"Now it came to pass, as He was praying in a certain place, when He ceased, that one of His disciples said to Him, "Lord teach us to pray, as John also taught his disciples." (Luke 11:1, NKJV)

One of my favorite game shows is, "Who Wants to be a Millionaire?" During this show, a person is asked a series of questions to attempt to win one million dollars. When someone is stuck on a question, they have the opportunity to reach out to three different lifelines. They can phone a friend, poll the audience for the answer, or they can have two of the wrong multiple choice answers removed. The person then has the opportunity to make a decision based on what that particular lifeline has revealed to them. Sometimes the lifeline works, other times...not so much.

The lifeline of an "Overcomer" is not a "hit or miss" like the lifelines of the game show. This is a lifeline that always gives the right answer and never misses a beat. We receive direction and guidance through our Lifeline.

"Overcomers" are always on top because they know how to activate their lifeline. Have you guessed it yet? Our lifeline is God, but it can only be activated through PRAYER! There are prayers at the end of each chapter because an "Overcomer" prays!

The simple definition of prayer is this: Communication and communion with God. We talk to God and then we listen while He talks to us. "Overcomers" commune with God because they desire His perfect will for their lives. If you ever want to be like someone or know what they know, you spend time with them. Prayer is a way of spending intimate quality time with God. Yes, when you pray you are speaking things, but you are also listening. Communication is a two-way street. God wants to share and reveal things with you in your prayer time with Him. Wondering if you should go someplace? Should you accept that job? Take that class? Pray! We have His heart not only by studying His word, but through prayer with Him.

I used to avoid things like praying in public or praying for large groups because I didn't think I prayed "well enough." Now, if that is not the craziest thing I don't know what is. In order to pray you do not have to use a lot of eloquent or fancy words, coupled with five, "Father God's" throughout your prayers. Imagine if you talked to your natural father in that way, "Dad, I need to go to the store. Dad get me some candy. Dad please get me some Gummi Bears. Dad, I thank you for doing it." Your father would probably look at you like you were crazy! It doesn't matter how loud you pray or how your voice sounds when you pray or how many times you say "Father God." None of that matters to God. What matters to God is that we come to Him with a pure heart.

━━━━━ ❧ ━━━━━

"Blessed are the pure in heart, for they shall see God." (Matthew 5:8, NKJV)

It doesn't matter how loud you pray or how your voice sounds... What matters to God is that we come to Him with a pure heart.

━━━━━━━━━━━

Let's not just take my word for it. Let's see what Jesus says about prayer.

In Luke 11:2-4 we see what is commonly referred to as the "Lord's Prayer." Nonetheless, what is referred to as the "Lord's Prayer" is actually a model that shows us "how" to pray. Reading these verses will also give you insight on what prayer should be accomplishing. Again, your prayers don't have to sound like the "Lord's prayer," yet this is a model that assists us in "how" we are too pray.

And he said unto them, When you pray, say, Our Father in heaven, hallowed be Your name Your kingdom come. Your will be done on earth as it is in heaven. Give us day by day our daily bread. And forgive us our sins, for we also forgive everyone who is indebted to us. And d o not lead us into temptation, but deliver us from the evil one. (Luke 11:2-4, NKJV)

Let's review these verses line by line. *"Our Father in heaven, hallowed be Your name, Your Kingdom come."* What we learn from this line is that when we come to God in prayer, we must first acknowledge who He is! He is God, the Great I am and we must recognize that! When we communicate with God, it's time to humble ourselves before Him. The way I do this is through thankfulness. What an awesome way to start prayer by just simply expressing your gratitude. We all can thank God for something. Even if you are having a rough time in life, the fact that you are able to read this book and breathe is something to be thankful about.

"Your will be done on earth as it is in heaven." This simply means that you desire God's will over your own personal agenda. What is God's will? Well, God's will definitely doesn't line up with sin. This means you can't pray that God blesses you with someone else's husband! Or you

can't pray that someone gets ran over by a car. If you want to make sure your prayer time isn't selfish, try praying for someone else's needs first! "Overcomers" show compassion for others through prayer. *"...Pray for one another, that you may be healed. The effective, fervent prayer of a righteous man much." (I Peter 5:16, NKJV)*

"Give us day by day our daily bread." This is acknowledgement of our daily need for God's presence and God's word which is substance for our souls. There is a gospel song that I love and some of the lyrics are, "...And I'm desperate for you, and I'm lost without you..." I love this song because I realize that without God's daily presence in my life, I am a sad, sad, person who is definitely lost. In prayer we should desire His presence, and expect to receive wisdom and comfort from God. This is our, "daily bread." Don't allow prayer to become ritualistic! This is a time of refreshing with "Our Father!" Get happy about the fact that you have a God who wants to commune with you!

"And forgive us our sins, for we also forgive everyone who is indebted to us." This goes back to the importance of Chapter 4, "Overcoming Hurt." We cannot expect to hear from God, or receive any wisdom from God if we come to Him with a heart of unforgiveness. Matthew

6:14-15 states, ***"For if you forgive men when they sin against you, your heavenly Father will also forgive you. But if you do not forgive men their sins, your father will not forgive your sins." (NKJV)*** In order to connect to our lifeline through prayer, we need God to be able to forgive our sins. Therefore we must put aside all strife, bitterness, and envy before we commune with our lifeline. Purpose yourself to release these things before coming to God in prayer. God isn't moving on the words of a "hater's" prayer. The hater's prayer is the one who comes to God but still has all of this hate and discord in their heart towards people. I used to wonder why certain prayers during my past were not being answered. Now I realize that during those times I was holding so much unforgiveness towards my natural father that I was blocking my own blessings.

   "And do not lead us into temptation, but deliver us from the evil one."   Lastly, Jesus is teaching us to be watchful of the enemy's plots, schemes, tricks, and temptations. In praying that God "delivers us from the evil one" we trust Him to expose, reveal, and remove those persons and situations that are not God's best for our lives. Jesus' death and resurrection from the cross means that we are already delivered from the evil one! Now we can just thank God for finished work!

In Christ we have the victory because He has overcome the world system! *"These things I have spoken to you that in Me you may have peace. In the world you will have tribulation; but be of good cheer, I have overcome the world." (John 16:33, NKJV)* The Bible does not say that we will never have problems. As a matter of fact it says that we will have "tribulation." However, the Bible then says for us to "be of good cheer, I have overcome the world!" When we pray, we can be confident and have peace knowing that everything is already ALRIGHT! We can smile and be cheerful knowing that our lifeline, Jesus Christ, has already overcome the world! And if Christ is in you, then you are an "Overcomer" too! "Overcomers," it is time to activate our lifeline! Let's get to praying!"

Prayer | Father, I thank you for who you are and for all you have done for me! As I enter into a posture of prayer give me a pure heart and renew in me a right spirit. For your Word says the pure at heart see God and I desire to see you in every area of my life. I desire to hear from you and experience your presence. Let my thoughts be your thoughts, your ways my ways. In Jesus' name, Amen.

Journal Exercise | ☺

Over the next few weeks, using what you have learned about prayer in this chapter, personalize the steps and apply them to your prayer life. Challenge yourself to spend at least 15 minutes a day in prayer for one week. You will find that as you become accustomed to being in God's presence by 5 minutes each additional week. Journal what God reveals to you during this time. This is the beginning of your personal prayer journal. As you review this journal weeks' from now, expect to see the evidence of prayers answered in your life.

_____
_____
_____
_____
_____
_____
_____
_____
_____
_____
_____
_____
_____
_____

Chapter 8

New Garments

Isaiah 61:3- "To grant [consolation and joy] to those who mourn in Zion--to give them an ornament (a garland or diadem) of beauty instead of ashes, the oil of joy instead of mourning, the garment [expressive] of praise instead of a heavy, burdened, and failing spirit--that they may be called oaks of righteousness [lofty, strong, and magnificent, distinguished for uprightness, justice, and right standing with God], the planting of the Lord, that He may be glorified." (Amplified)

Tears begin to flow as I felt complete anguish from a broken heart. It had happened again, and the tears were flowing because I thought I knew better. I knew that being in this particular relationship was not God's best for me. Yet, I allowed my emotions to put me in a place where now I wished I could turn back the hands of time. I just wanted the pain to go away. I longed for that sour feeling in my stomach to disappear. And then, for the first time in a very long time, I literally cried out to God and worshipped Him. Can you believe all of this was taking place in my car as I was driving to work one morning? I did not care who was looking from the other cars, I just poured out my heart to God. I told God how much I loved Him, how much I needed Him and I just thanked Him for being who He is! The presence of God began to fall on me in the car and translated into one of the most unforgettable worship experiences of my life. At that point I realized how to wear the "Garment of Praise."

Jesus hugged me that day. And as peculiar as that may sound, He did. No one can heal a broken heart like Jesus! ***Psalms 147:3 says, "He heals the brokenhearted and binds up their wounds." (NIV)*** However the way to access this healing is by putting on this "Garment of Praise."The Garment of Praise" is simply accessed through our worship! Joy and peace are like buttons on this garment. They attached to our praise. At that time in my life the Holy Spirit comforted me like never before because I invited him in through sincere worship and praise.

When we go through challenging periods in our lives, so often we run to people for advice, pouring out our hearts to them, crying on their shoulders, and getting hugs from them. At times this is helpful to us and it seems convenient. Yet, even when we do this, we have to remember that "we" can ask our Heavenly Father, who is our friend and our comforter, for all of these things. Praise paralyzes the enemy! When we praise and worship God, picture Satan immobile and paralyzed! He cannot move when you praise! We can cry out to God, invoke His presence and He will give us what we need. I know because that day, and many days during periods of intimate praise and worship, I received what I needed. "Overcomers" wear the "Garment of Praise," and because of this, they are healed, restored and made whole in Him.

That day when I experienced that heartbreak, it was revealed to me that God is not only a healer, a restorer, and a redeemer, but he is *my* healer, *my* restorer, and *my* redeemer. Although His blood was shed for all of us, it became clear that he died for ME! You have to make this thing personal!

Say this aloud!

"Jesus died for ME! Because of this, I am healed, I am restored, I am an Overcomer! Christ died for my pain, so that I can have joy! I will have joy, I will walk peaceably, and I will love my life!"

Regardless of your past, because you are in a covenant relationship with Christ, you can come boldly to the throne of grace and receive His mercy. ***Hebrews 4:16- Let us therefore come boldly unto the throne of grace that we may obtain mercy, and find grace to help in time of need.*** In your time of need there is a loving Father, who is waiting to lift your heavy burdens, and give you beauty for ashes, through your Praise.

Prayer | Thank you, Father, for allowing me to experience your presence through the promised gift of the Holy Spirit. I thank you for sending your son Jesus to die, so that I can put on a "Garment of Praise," and rejoice instead of mourn. You are the healer of hearts and my redeemer! Your mercy and grace are everlasting! Thank you for making me whole and complete in you! In Jesus' name I pray, Amen.

Journal Exercise | ☺

Today, I want you to practice your worship. Pick a quiet place, a place that you are comfortable in. If it takes for you to put on a worship CD, then do that. Try worshipping God for at least 5 minutes alone today. You may want to do it longer and that's great! If you don't know what to do or say, begin by just telling God how you are thankful for Him. Close your eyes if you need too in order to focus. Focus on His goodness towards you! Focus on His love! After you've done this, how did you feel? What did God say to you if anything? Record your experience in the space allotted.

Chapter 9

The Key to Total Transformation- A New Mindset

Therefore, I urge you, brothers and sisters, in view of God's mercy, to offer your bodies as a living sacrifice, holy and pleasing to God—this is your true and proper worship. [2] Do not conform to the pattern of this world, but be transformed by the renewing of your mind. Then you will be able to test and approve what God's will is—his good, pleasing and perfect will. (Romans 12:1-2, NIV)

When my lifestyle changed the words I would often hear were, "They must have brainwashed you down at that church." When I became serious about God my words began to change, along with my actions. Considering my experience, I realize that if the truth is to be told, many of us need our brains washed. Why? I'm sure you are wondering.

Day in and day out through media, friends, family, and other sources, our minds have become tainted. We see images and ideas about life that do not truly reflect the Kingdom of God and His order. In order to live an

"Overcomer's" lifestyle, we have to renew our minds! This will allow us to truly walk in God's will which is "good, acceptable, and perfect!"

In the verse above Paul charges us in the book of Romans to offer our bodies as a living sacrifice unto God. He then gives us instructions on how to do this very thing. Many of us cannot stop cursing, having sex out of marriage, or lying, simply because we refuse to do the work of renewing our minds. Although this may be a hard pill to swallow, where you are today is a result of your mindset.

We live in a world where it's "normal" for women to dress slutty and have sex with whoever they want. We live in a world where it's "normal" for men to sing and rap about sex on the radio and describe in detail what they will do to a woman. So what does that mean? It means we must change our "normal" to line up with God's word. Society's norm does not have to be your norm. In order to be an "Overcomer" we must resist the urge to conform to the negativity we see in society.

At one point in my life it was normal for me to drink, smoke, engage in sexual acts with the same sex and/or the opposite sex, curse because I was "expressing myself," dress any type of way; I mean the list can go on. However, when I made a decision to live for Christ, some things had to change. Number one on the list after making a decision for salvation was to renew my mind. Just because my spirit changed overnight didn't mean my mind did. This was going to take work because now I had to work on purging years of negative behaviors out of my mind, and turn them into positive.

"If that animal blood and the other rituals of purification were effective in cleaning up certain matters of our religion and behavior, think how much more the blood of Christ cleans up our whole lives, inside and out. Through the Spirit, Christ offered himself as an unblemished sacrifice, freeing us from all those dead-end efforts to make ourselves respectable, so that we can live all out for God." (Hebrews 9: 13-14, Message Bible)

Back in the day, before Jesus Christ came to die for our sins, men used rituals that included sacrificing animals unto God in order to purify themselves. However, we have the better deal now since we are in Christ. His blood sacrifice on the cross gives us the ability to live the life of an "Overcomer!" When Jesus died on the cross for us, he placed the ball in our court! The power is now in our hands to live the life He intends for us to have through a renewed mind!

In 2005 when I decided to make a decision to renew my mind, there were some steps that I took in order to begin the mind renewal process!

First, I committed to a Bible believing, Bible teaching church! I committed to attending a ministry that was teaching the word of God in simplicity so that I could apply the Word into my daily life. It also helped to be around other believers who could encourage and assist me in my new faith walk. *"Not forsaking or neglecting to assemble together [as believers], as is the habit of some people, but admonishing (warning, urging, and encouraging) one another, and all the more faithfully as you see the day approaching."*(Hebrews 10:25, Amplified Version) Through this commitment to being at a church, I began to serve and volunteer in the ministry.

Second, I began to serve others as I was renewing my mind. This allowed me to be around more people who had my answers instead of my problems because of the new relationships that formed through serving. It also helped me to focus on other's needs greater than my own, and develop character.

Third, I evaluated my "relationships." This included friendships. As stated in the chapter, "What About Your

Friends," our relationships are critical to our development as a believer. During the mind renewal process you will recognize that you will have to evaluate and possibly change your interactions with certain friends. If I were to now believe that having sex outside of marriage was wrong, I could not engage as much in conversations with those who did not have a problem with it. If I wanted to stand strong with certain Biblical beliefs, the majority of my interactions needed to be with people who were going in a similar direction.

> *If I wanted to stand strong with certain Biblical beliefs, the majority of my interactions needed to be with people who were going in a similar direction.*

Lastly, I monitored what I allowed myself to watch and listen too. *"Above all else, guard your heart, for everything you do flows from it."* (Proverbs 4:23, NIV) There were certain types of music that I could no longer listen to or certain movies that I could no longer watch. I monitored how certain music or how certain movies/television shows made me feel, or what I began to think as I entertained myself with them. For example, there was a certain song by an attractive rap artist that I used to like! I mean the beat was HOT! Yet, when I listened to the song, my mind would wander and I would think about sex! There are certain movies that I have not seen to this day because people have told me about their wild sex scenes. As I am writing this book, I am engaged to a fine man of God and I have been celibate since July of 2005! Listening or watching these types of things will not help me stay this course. I would be lying to you if I said the thought of sex doesn't come in my mind; however my mind is never flooded with these types of things because I properly guard what goes before my eyes and into my ears. Furthermore, once I began to guard what went into my ears and eyes, I strategically flooded my ears and eyes with music and programs that were edifying and positive. For one entire year I did not listen to any secular or worldly music. Now I'm not saying that has to be your route. This was just something I felt I needed to do in order to help renew my mind so that I can have a totally transformed life.

As you go on with the task of renewing your mind so that you can live and walk in the "good, acceptable, and perfect" will of God, you will have to be honest with yourself. You can personally identify things in your life that are hindering your thinking from going to the next level. Let's recap these mind renewing tips: Find a Bible believing,

Bible teaching church that teaches the word of God in a way that you can understand and apply; evaluate your relationships/friendships and change them if necessary; begin to serve and/or volunteer in areas of ministry that interest you; and guard your heart by protecting what goes in your ears and what you watch. As we've learned in Chapter 4, Controlling Your Thoughts, "whatever you think on in abundance, will expand." Your thoughts and your mindset will set your life in a negative or positive direction. The choice is up to you! Now that you've learned how to control your thoughts, by *"taking captive every thought to make it obedient to Christ"* (2 Corinthians 10:5, NIV) go even further by continuing to develop the Godly mindset that will set you on the course of a blessed life! Now let's put the Word into practice, and watch yourself overcome negative mindsets!

Prayer | *Father, thank you for cleansing my mind from all things that do not glorify you. Continue to give me a servant's heart, and as I'm serving surround me with Godly counsel that will positively influence my life. Expose, reveal, and remove those in my life who do not have my best interest at heart. As I fill my mind according to Your word in Philippians 4:8 with things that are good, and pure, give me an even greater understanding of your Word. Give me the wisdom to effectively guard my heart and mind so that I can be in an even better position to serve you. In Jesus Name I pray, Amen.*

Journal Exercise | ☺

ﾑ *Do your research. If you do not currently belong to a church, began to identify churches in your immediate area that you believe are Bible teaching churches. Prayerfully compile your list of at least 3, and make it a point to visit those churches within the next 6 months.*

ﾑ *Began to serve on a small scale. If you're not already, find a ministry within your church (or a church that you frequent) that lines up with your interests. If youth is your passion, sign up to help out with an upcoming event. Doing this will help to take your mind off of your problems, while still making an impact in the body of Christ.*

ﾑ *Evaluate one of your relationships. Make a list of at least 3 friends that you think could be blocking you from having an effective relationship with Jesus Christ. Now that you've made your list, here comes the hard part. Call up one of the friends on your list. Talk to them about your journey to get closer to God and gage their general reaction. Again, this may be a long process, as some of us have had certain friends for decades, but an immediate clue that you might need to eliminate a friendship, is if they have a negative reaction to your new walk in Christ.*

ﾑ *List, list, list. Make a list of the top 5 television shows, books, songs etc that you think may be hindrance in your walk with Christ. If you can quit watching/listening to these cold turkey, go for it! If not, make a commitment to giving up at least one thing each week. The process is gradual, but the results will be hugely beneficial!*

Chapter 10

Pursuing Purpose With Passion

Jeremiah 29:11- For I know the plans I have for you," says the Lord. "They are plans for good and not for disaster, to give you a future and a hope. (New Living Translation) Habakkuk 2:2-3- And then God answered: "Write this. Write what you see. Write it out in big block letters so that it can be read on the run. This vision-message is a witness pointing to what's coming. It aches for the coming—it can hardly wait! And it doesn't lie. If it seems slow in coming, wait. It's on its way. It will come right on time. (Message Bible)

When I look over my past I realize that many of the destructive things I did was because I had no sense of purpose. Not only did I not know who I was in Christ, I did not have any clear direction or vision for my life. All I knew was that I was to go to school, get good grades, go to college, so I can get a good job, work many years, and then collect retirement from my investments and the government. Does this sound familiar to you? As I grew to know God and experience the blessing of living right, this routine way of living was no longer "comfortable" to me. I knew that there had to be something more out of life. I had begun to understand my "overall" purpose in Christ. Overall, we as believers according to God's word are called to be the "salt of the earth" and the "light of the world."

> *"You are the salt of the earth. But if the salt loses its saltiness, how can it be made salty again? It is no longer good for anything, except to be thrown out and trampled underfoot. You are the light of the world. A town built on a hill cannot be hidden." (Matthew 5:13-14, NIV)*

This basically means that we are to literally be extensions of Christ in the earth. We are to show His glory and love all people. People should be able to look into our lives that do not know God and have an encounter with Jesus because of Him being in us. I can tell you there were many times in my past with the bad attitude I struggled with, that people saw anyone but Jesus. Yet, as salt brings flavor to your food, we are to bring flavor to the world! What does that mean you might ask? When something has flavor it is not plain, or boring. It makes whatever you are eating taste better. Well just as a great seasoning can make some food taste better; we who are the salt of the earth should make the lives of those around us better. The truth is many people are miserable and don't make the lives of others better because they are not walking in their "specific" purpose! In this chapter you will see me use the words "specific" or "divine" purpose. This simply means, what God specifically has called you to do here on this earth. We are called to produce positive change, to be the light of the world, and ultimately glorify God. But how are you specifically called to do this? Knowing the answer to that question has the ability to bring you great fulfillment. There is no feeling like walking in your purpose. It's great to wake up knowing that there's no other thing in the world that you would like to be doing, and that you are great at what you do! Now in my dreams I would sound like CeCe Winans and sing all over the world. The anointing in my voice would cause people to want to worship God. Nonetheless, if I am to sing anything it will probably make you want to run away rather than worship. It is obvious that this is not my specific purpose in life, I am not called to do it, and I am terrible at it. God doesn't love me any less than he does CeCe! He just gave me different gifts to operate in that are a part of "my" specific purpose.

At 11 years old I was graduating from Whittier Elementary School and was the M.C. of the graduation program. The teachers always put me before audiences to speak during our assemblies. Yet this was extra special to me because I was graduating and going to the 7th grade! During the program, it was a time where the parents and participants were talking loudly as we were trying to transition. I stood there at the podium, about 4 feet tall, and I said to the audience, "I'll wait!" The looks on those adults' faces were priceless. Not only did I command their attention, but I was 11 years old and I spoke with such boldness it startled them. My mother said in the audience people were wondering who this little girl is thought she was. Now although I commanded the audience with a little "sassiness" my great-grandmother saw something else. After my graduation she pulled me aside and told me that I would be a great speaker one day. That I would one day speak to audiences' across the world. My great-grandmother saw one of my gifts that day and that gift was to command the attention of an audience through speaking. She saw into my specific purpose here on this earth. She saw me operate in something that was better than a lot of children and adults, with boldness, and with ease. Although I had the gift of public speaking at that age, it needed to be perfected, and trained. Over the years of my life I have worked to do just that and today I am comfortable speaking to audiences, and I now know how to speak to them without getting too sassy.

There are 3 keys I will share with you that have helped me to walk in my "specific" or "divine" purpose and I believe that they will be a blessing to you as well.

Three Keys | Walking in Specific Purpose

The first step is to ***spend time with God.*** You may be saying, "Well that's what I'm doing now as I'm reading this book." "God is always with me, so I'm always spending time with him." "I go to church on Sunday and for Bible studies." Well all of these things may be true, but have you spent time alone with God specifically as it relates to your purpose? I've had to check myself in this area from time to time. I was doing "ministry work" I was even reading or studying the Bible for a Bible college assignment. However, this cannot replace spending quality time with God to allow Holy Spirit to speak to you. God truly wants to reveal our purpose to us so that we may glorify Him in what we do, and draw people to Him. Many times we cannot hear God because our mind is running a marathon. If you haven't already, I suggest setting aside some quiet time with the Lord where you can pray, reflect, and just collect your thoughts. My pastor Dr. Michael Freeman has often stated, "Favor is hidden in the voice of God, found in the obedience of His instructions." Spending time with God is the only way we can become developed in hearing His voice to receive instructions. Often times, to receive more understanding regarding our purpose, there are instructions that God may want us to complete before revealing the next set. Before I knew I would write a book, or minister on this level I received one instruction from God and

Spending time with God is the only way we can become developed in hearing His voice to receive instructions.

that was to attend Spirit of Faith Bible Institute. After I obeyed that instruction, I began to receive more clarity from God on steps I was to take towards my purpose. The point is this, we can never expect to receive information, instructions, or clarity regarding what God has called us to do if we do not purpose ourselves to spend quality time with Him.

With the spiritual directions there are also some natural clues that we should look for that will give us insight into our purpose. For the second step, I have included a list of questions I want you to ask yourself about something that you may feel that you are called to do. Whether it is to write, preach, or practice medicine, ***ask yourself these questions below:***

- ❧ ***Is this fun to me? Do I enjoy it?***
- ❧ ***Can I do this all day?***
- ❧ ***Am I happy doing this even without getting paid what I desire at first?***
- ❧ ***Do I have a desire to learn about this particular thing I enjoy? Do I enjoy becoming better at it?***
- ❧ ***Do I talk about this thing all the time, and enjoy sharing information about it with others?***

If you've answered yes to all of these questions, chances are you may have identified something that you are specifically or called to do.

Once you have identified that particular "thing" that you've answered "yes" too in the second step you are then ready for the third step. The third step will be beneficial to continue for the rest of your life. The reason why this step is something that you will continue for the remainder of your life is because we are always evolving and growing. The third step involves ***creating a Vision Map, or a "Purpose Blueprint."*** Before an architect goes on to build a structure, he carefully plans with other developers a blueprint for the project. The blueprint is very specific and serves as a guide that helps the builders create the vision. Your personal Vision Map will be your Purpose Blueprint to help guide you and keep you on course. Writing down your goals, ideas, and visions not only helps you to keep record of them, but they serve as a way of holding you accountable to your own words. "Overcomers" who are pursuing their purpose with passion give themselves thorough evaluations of where they are, where they desire to be, and what it will take in order to get there. At the end of the year, you should be able to look back and see what was accomplished through the instructions you've received from spending time with God, and the goals you've set for yourself.

In the next few pages, the journal exercise includes various areas in which you can begin creating your Vision Map-Purpose Blueprint. There are also instructions on how to create a Vision Board. A Vision Board is a tool to go along with your written goals and serves as a visual stimulator. Creating a vision board will help you to actually "see" what you are working towards on a daily basis.   "Overcomer" Congratulations on taking the necessary steps to fulfill your Divine Purpose.   Overcomers make impact! Overcomers have flavor! Overcomers walk in Purpose!

Prayer | Father, I thank you for perfecting all things that concern me. Lord as I mediate on your Word and spend time with you, I ask that you continue to reveal how I am to serve you here on this earth. Your Word says the steps of a good man are ordered by you, and I thank you in advance for ordering each of my steps; as I purpose to walk in the calling that you have ordained for me. I ask for your guidance as I begin to set goals, and create a Vision Map. All of these things I thank you for. In Jesus Name, Amen.

Journal Exercise | ☺

VISION |
Definition: a: something seen in a dream, trance, especially: a supernatural appearance that conveys a revelation b: a thought, concept, or object formed by the imagination c: a manifestation to the senses of something immaterial 2 a: the act or power of imagination b (1): mode of seeing or conceiving (2): unusual discernment or foresight c: direct awareness of the supernatural usually in visible form3 a: the act or power of seeing.

"God has given us clear instructions to write down our visions, desires and dreams, because at the appointed time, they will manifest in our lives. Writing will provide a means of recording the things you desire from God. God has given us another form of writing the vision, beyond mere pen and paper. "(Dr. Lindsay Marsh-Warren, Author of The Best Sex of My Life, A Guide to Purity).

Describe the vision for your life. The next few pages in the journal are separated into various sections to help you organize your visions: school, career, family, friendships, physical (lifting weights, exercise, eating right), extracurricular activities (sports, computers, etc.), and spiritual (church attendance, ministry, etc.).

SPIRITUAL GOALS |
II Timothy 2:15-Do your best to present yourself to God as one approved, a worker who has no need to be ashamed, rightly handling the word of truth. (English Standard Version)

_____

_____

_____

_____

_____

_____

_____

_____

SCHOOL/EDUCATION RELATED GOALS |

Proverbs 20:11-Even a child is known by his actions, by whether his conduct is pure and right. (New International Version)

_____

_____

_____

_____

_____

_____

_____

CAREER GOALS |

Jeremiah 29:11-For I know the plans I have for you," declares the LORD, "plans to prosper you and not to harm you, plans to give you hope and a future. (New International Version)

_____

_____

_____

_____

_____

_____

_____

FAMILY & RELATIONSHIP GOALS |

Matthew 15:4-Didn't God command you to respect your father and mother? (Contemporary English Version) Colossians 3:20- "Children, do what your parents tell you. This delights the Master no end." (Message Bible)

_____
_____
_____
_____
_____
_____
_____

FRIENDSHIP GOALS |

Proverbs 18:24- A man who has friends must himself be friendly, But there is a friend who sticks closer than a brother. (New King James Version)

_____
_____
_____
_____
_____
_____

PHYSICAL GOALS |

I Corinthians 6:19-You surely know that your body is a temple where the Holy Spirit lives. The Spirit is in you and is a gift from God. You are no longer your own. (Contemporary English Version)

_____

_____

_____

_____

_____

_____

_____

EXTRACURRICULAR GOALS |

Romans 8:29-And we know that in all things God works for the good of those who love him, who have been called according to his purpose. (New International Version)

_____

_____

_____

_____

_____

_____

_____

HOW TO CREATE A VISION BOARD |
Materials Needed
- ✓ *Magazines, Books, Newspaper Headlines*
- ✓ *Construction Paper or Cork Board*
- ✓ *Scissors, Glue*

Using what you have written in your journal under the various sections about goals, begin to search for photos in books, magazines, or newspapers that directly relates to your goal. For example if my goal is to become fit by joining a gym a photo I would look for maybe someone exercising. Also look for various "buzz words" and phrases within the magazines that will motivate you to complete your goals. For example if my goal is to manage my money better, I may cut out buzz words that have something to do with financial empowerment, budgeting, investing, or saving. (Jennifer at one of my Purpose Parties with her completed "Purpose Blueprint").

Chapter 11

The Overcomer's Confession

I have created this confession specifically for you! Write your name in the blank space and make this personal. Because words have such great power, I encourage you to continually speak words of life over yourself. No matter what you've been told you are beautiful, and wonderful in God's eyes. *{Psalm 139:14, "I praise you because I am fearfully and wonderfully made; your works are wonderful, I know that full well."}* As you confess these words over your life, allow them to become alive in your soul. There was once a time where my self-esteem was in the pits! As you know from the introduction I didn't like much of anything about myself. I hated the way I looked, and was ashamed of what I've been through. It was through positive confession that the outlook of myself began to change. I would post confessions on my mirror and as I was getting ready for work I would read the confessions aloud. You have to literally speak yourself into a positive self image. We must speak positive about ourselves until we believe it.

(Your Name Goes Here) is a virtuous woman of God according to Proverbs 31. My tongue is controlled by the law of kindness, my speech filled with grace and wisdom. I Peter 2:9 describe my identity. This means I am a chosen generation, royalty, holy, and God's special woman set apart for divine purpose. With the wisdom of God, I build in my life what God has designed for me in Heaven. My heart is pure towards God therefore I see God in every area of my life. I draw near to God and he draws near to me; because of this everything that I do, touch, or am involved in prospers. I do not judge others by their appearance but with righteous judgment. This means I pray for and share Christ to those in need. I am not involved in gossip or tale bearing. I keep my word and people can trust me. I walk in love, even with my enemies knowing God fights my battles therefore, I always win. If God is before me, who can be against me? My body is for the Lord and the Lord for my body that means I do not engage in any immoral acts. I am free from all perversions and any generational curses as I present my body a living sacrifice holy and acceptable unto God. I am the light of the world, an Overcomer, a World Changer, a righteous, virtuous woman. My value is high, I am worthy of God's best, and I will have God's best in my life. I am made whole according to my faith and win in every area of my life! In Jesus' name, Amen!

Journal Exercise | ☺

Use the next few pages to continue to write positive confessions and affirmations for various areas of your life. (self-esteem, finances, relationship with family, school, employment) Write down the things you want to see in these areas. Write them in the present tense as if you already are walking in what you desire. An "Overcomer" always speaks faith filled words!

_____

_____

_____

_____

_____

_____

_____

_____

_____

Chapter 12

Ten Quick Overcomer Tips!

These are 10 quick "Overcomer" tips for the woman on the go! I encourage you to keep this book/journal with you at all times to reflect upon the things God spoke to you through this book. We all need "quick" inspiration from time to time. When the pressure is on at work, when you feel like you want to blow, when the tears well up in your eyes, come to this page for your quick boost of encouragement!

1. Make sure you keep your heart pure. Always check out your motives. When your motivation is LOVE you will begin to see God's hand on your life. The Pure at Heart See God. **Matthew 5:8** *Blessed are the pure in heart: for they shall see God.*

2. Begin to Renew your Mind so you will discover "truth." o John 8:31-32 (Amplified Bible)-31So Jesus said to those Jews who had believed in Him, If you abide in My word [hold fast to My teachings and live in accordance with them], you are truly My disciples. 32And you will know the Truth, and the Truth will set you free. Romans 12:2 **(KJV)**And be not conformed to this world: but be ye transformed by the renewing of your mind, that ye may prove what is that good, and acceptable, and perfect, will of God.

3. Get with those who have your answer, get away from those who have your problems. (Words of Dr. Michael Freeman). **2 Corinthians 6:14 (KJV)** Be ye not unequally yoked together with unbelievers: for what fellowship hath righteousness with unrighteousness? and what communion hath light with darkness?

4. Speak the Word over your life on a consistent basis. Use your mouth and the Word of God which is your weapon! **Hebrews 4:12 (Contemporary English Version)** What God has said isn't only alive and active! It is sharper than any double-edged sword. His word can cut through our spirits and souls and through our joints and marrow, until it discovers the desires and thoughts of our hearts. **Ephesians 6:17** And take the helmet of salvation, and the sword of the Spirit, which is the word of God: **Proverbs 18:21** Death and life are in the power of the tongue: and they that love it shall eat the fruit thereof.

5. *Get in a Bible Teaching, Bible Believing Church Home!* **Hebrews 10:25 (Amplified Bible)** *Not forsaking or neglecting to assemble together [as believers], as is the habit of some people, but admonishing (warning, urging, and encouraging) one another, and all the more faithfully as you see the day approaching.*

6. *Recognize that you are a new creature in Christ and be determined to walk in that newness!* **II Corinthians 5:17** *(Don't allow people to tell you any different.)*

7. *Recognize that the same Power that raised Jesus from the dead is the same power that is within you when you accept Him!* **Philippians 4:13**

8. *Know that God Loves You! When you repent (turn away) from sin, he remembers them no more! Don't allow the guilt and condemnation from the enemy keep you from coming to Christ!* **Zephaniah 3:17 (Amplified Bible)** *The Lord your God is in the midst of you, a Mighty One, a Savior [Who saves]! He will rejoice over you with joy; He will rest [in silent satisfaction] and in His love He will be silent and make no mention [of past sins, or even recall them]; He will exult over you with singing.* **Romans 5:8 (Amplified Bible)** *But God*

shows and clearly proves His [own] love for us by the fact that while we were still sinners, Christ (the Messiah, the Anointed One) died for us.

9. Seek to develop spiritually daily! **(Psalm 1:1-3, Joshua 1:8, II Tim 2:15)** This is necessary for us to overcome trials, tests, and temptations. We need the word to be IN us, so when the test comes what will come out of us is the Word! Meditating on the word day and night is the key to success in every area of our life! Including living a life of purity!

10. Seek FIRST always the Kingdom! **(Matthew 6:33)** A big mistake many people make is to focus on the problem and not the solution. The answer to any pain we've experienced in our past is simply in Jesus. He died so that we can be free! When we take our focus off the fact that things may not be going the way we'd like them at this time and focus on developing this relationship with God; steps are being taken in the right direction. These steps will lead to wholeness in Christ! Seek first the Kingdom of God and HIS righteousness, and as the Word of God says, "all things" will be added unto you! This means every great thing that lies within God's perfect will for your life.

Acknowledgments

There are many people who made this book possible and I am forever grateful for everything that you've given, and poured into my life to make it possible. You have been an integral part of this vision coming to past. First I must thank my Lord and Savior Jesus Christ! God is beyond amazing and Lord this book is to glorify you! I would also like to thank my parents {Gregory and Robin Schumpert} for all of their prayers and encouragement along the way. Thank you for being my best friends and being great parents. I thank my fiancé (who will be my husband by 9/24/11) Jeffrey Tyler for pushing the vision God has given me and for being my biggest coach! I love you so much! I am thankful for his parents the "Sidberry's" for your prayers, consistent love & encouragement. A special thank you to my pastors Drs. Mike and Dee Dee Freeman of the Spirit of Faith Christian Center! Thank you for the Word of Faith that you pour into my life and for being loving pastors! Clearly I have the best pastors in the world!! ☺ Thank you Leonard Poteat for being such an awesome support and designing an amazing bookcover; while doing photoshoots for me every other month! LOL Vianca Smith, you are the best MUA ever and a great friend! Thanks for hooking my "cover" look up! Kellie Thompson, my friend, fellow author, and stylist, I'm so grateful for our weekly encouragement talks. You have uplifted me in so many ways. Love you girl! Thank you Erica Pitts for your editing! You did an amazing job and are a gifted editor. Pastor Tracie Millard, I appreciate you reviewing some of the chapters and for being a blessing to me! Thanks to my brother Ricardo Owens for all of our talks of encouragement and your love. To my East of the River Clergy, Police, Community Partnership family, FREE Ministry, and Worth the Wait Family, particularly Dr. Lindsay Marsh-Warren I thank you for all of your love and encouragement along the way. Thank you Dr. Ty Adams for your encouragement, inspiration and support. To the ladies of My Virtuositee, you rock! Shaun and Ana Saunders this was truly a holy hook up! I am a proud member now of the Godzchild Publication family and I am honored! I cannot thank you guys enough! Special thanks to Alana McCarter for introducing me to this awesome publisher, and being the most "Positive" woman I know! To Geneen Cross, thank you for your personal support along the way. Tiffany Green and Tamika Cambridge, you've inspired me as partners in purpose, thank you! Brelyn Freeman, thank you for your heart to just be a blessing! You are a walking inspiration of what Faith can do! Thanks for your consistent support! To "ALL of my family and friends," you know who you are, I appreciate and thank you for your words of encouragement and support along the way! There are so many of you who love and support me and I could write another book thanking you all! ☺

Last but not least, I must give a very special thanks to my **Publication Partners!** Without you, this would not be possible at this time in my life. Every seed you have sown I pray that it produces a great harvest in your own life. I pray that every vision you have for your life comes to past! You all have blessed me in more ways than you will ever know! *(Nikieta Lea, Jocelyn Saunders, Shalonda Perry, LaQuanda Washington, Armond Mosley, Lanita Wilks, Rahiel Tesfamariam, Crystal Moohn, Dr. MA Lee, Amanda Porter, Kalilia D Wilson, Sherri Colbert, Jeffrey Tyler, Mignon Broughton, Tiffany Jackson, Laetitia Lukanda, Sherri Colbert, Tricia Jones, Darius Brown, Jazmin Smith, Kelli Oldham, Eric Chapman, Autumn & Terry Joiner, Tiffany Edmunds, Ray Wright)*

Jennifer Lucy

Jennifer Lucy is a young woman who has discovered her life's purpose is to empower, and encourage others by providing them the tools they need to discover their purpose and ultimately walk in wholeness. Her personal story is one that began with struggle yet she overcomes by faith; has continued with perseverance, and ultimately success; to see the manifestation of her dreams. She attended DC public schools and is a graduate of Spirit of Faith Bible Institute where she has been "trained to carry out her God ordained assignment with excellence, integrity, and with a spirit of faith."

Upon completion of this program she received a Diploma of Ministerial Studies. Currently she is studying Theology and Leadership at Regent University. She is also a licensed minister at the Spirit of Faith Christian Center Church where she worships and serves with two outreach based ministries. Jennifer began motivational speaking in 2006. Since 2006 she has been speaking at various non-profits, panels, conferences, universities, and churches across the nation.

In 2009 she partnered with 2 of her friends to form the company Unleashing Potential LLC. This organization specializes in Purpose and Leadership Development, as well as women and youth empowerment. Some of her workshops to date have been "Pursuing Purpose with Passion," "The Mind & Heart of a Princess," "Fearfully and Wonderfully Made," and "Sexology."

She is also a model and volunteer for the Worth the Wait organization founded by her mentor Dr. Lindsay Marsh-Warren. Her writing has been featured in Jubilee Magazine's July 2008 issue, and WOW Magazine 2008/2009 Winter edition. For more information on Jennifer Lucy regarding booking information, her books, and workshops please go to www.jenniferlucyinspires.com. For personal enjoyment Jennifer is a blogger at http://jenniferlucyinspires.com/blog, she loves to empower others through writing, travel, model, read, and shop!